GW01417639

The Slumbering Pines

The following poems have previously been published online on the Write Loud website:
Beyond the Trees, A Quiet Man, I Want, Moon shadows, The Old Vanity Case, Nan's Lippy,
Drama, The Fledgling, The Fox Visited Me Last Night, Under the Stairs.

Copyright of all the above poems and all poems in totality in this book remain the property of the author.

ISBN: 9781729165775

The Slumbering Pines Copyright © 2018 Taylor Crowshaw
Cover Copyright © 2018 Taylor Crowshaw

All rights reserved. This book, or parts thereof, may not be reproduced or
transmitted in any form or by any means, electronic or mechanical,
including recording, photocopying, offset, or by any information storage
and retrieval system without permission in writing from the author, except
by reviewers who may quote brief passages to be printed in a magazine or
newspaper.

Contents

Introduction

Look beyond the trees

into this book of poetry.

It is where you will find

poems of every kind.

Poetic stories told in rhyme,

to mesmerise and take your time.

Verses short and sweet for a treat.

Funny little rhymes to tickle your ears.

Poems about donkeys, trees and birds,

and one about spiders under the stairs.

There is something to read for everyone,

so please enjoy and have some fun.

Taylor.

© 2018 Taylor Crowshaw

Part One - Letting Go

A Quiet Man

She sat among strangers, discarded pamphlets strewn everywhere.
A face smiling up at her from a photo on a chair.
Handsome and young, she could not leave him abandoned.

As his friend of many years had sat waiting a few days before,
his love, his wife would not answer his call.
Children left unaware that soon he would no longer be there,
as his friend sat waiting outside on a chair.

Recalling her sorrow that he had died all alone,
handkerchief to her eyes as she sits on her own.
For this quiet man... her friend of many years,
she struggled to stifle her sobs and her tears.

Few words were uttered, and words of mourning muttered.
She had wanted to stand and regale with tales of his life,
but could not, would not usurp his children and wife.
So little was said of his life on that day,
before the mourners moved slowly away.

A room filled with laughter would not be his way,
he would not have requested bright colours to celebrate his life.

Just a quiet sobriety, and the tears of his friend, his children and wife.

© 2018 Taylor Crowshaw

Standing at the Station

The train pulls into the station., too soon,
they hold hands in the waiting room.
Duffle bag slung casually over his right shoulder,
his mother wishing, he was a little older.

Why is it they wonder that he joined up,
undisciplined they called him a young pup.
Off to train... on the train.
Nothing to lose so much to gain.

Slowly as the train left the station
she turned and faced his mother.
Heartbroken bereft torn apart,
to her there was no other.

Every week she would queue outside the red telephone box,
waiting for his words and the emotions they would unlock.
Letters written with regularity to each other.
Jeers and sarcasm upon their arrival, from her brother.

Every three months a stolen weekend
when her broken heart could temporarily mend.
Mundane tasks to keep her from thinking.
She was never one for drinking.

She would visit his parents' house feeling connected,
sitting were he often would sit.
If she closed her eyes his presence she could feel,
although in her heart she knew it was never real.

After a while he passed out... they saw the parade,
on that day plans for their future were made.
They would get married the following year.
He told her they would be together forever, and never to fear.

She often watches the train leaving the station,
a young man looks back with a smile on his face,
of the fear he would have to face, there is not a trace.

He arrived back home one day on that train,
he could not smile and jump off to greet her.
Solemnly he was carried off in a box,
like many others to them he was lost.

How many years it took they do not know,

but one day they knew it would be time to let go.

Those memories now locked. Deep inside her mind.

Time to move on but never forget,

and when they remember and call him to mind think of him fondly and

always be kind.

© 2018 Taylor Crowshaw

What's the Hurry?

People rushing everywhere,
no time to stop no time to spare.
There is no time to sit and ponder,
or through life to wander.

Hurry here hurry there,
people hurry everywhere.
Life these days moves so fast,
we wonder how can it last.

Do not try to stop and talk,
look away and quickly walk.
Unless you are offering money,
then just walk away honey.

Tapping fingers in a queue,
huffing and puffing behind you.
No patience to stop and wait.
Look at the time... going to be late.

Take a breath, look around,
the beauty of life is profound.
Do not put it off and wait.

Before you know... it will be too late.

© 2018 Taylor Crowshaw

Memories

Woolen mittens cover chilblained hands,
tears before bed Mother understands.
A black gabardine mac.
Walnuts in a bowl by the fire to crack.

Frosted window panes greet the morning light,
as the dawn of the day replaces the night.
A winter wonderland for small fingernails to scrape.
Whilst a shivering Mother has the breakfast to make.

Covers pulled up quickly, over a wet bed.
Tears, as to the table the children are led.
Reading the back of the cereal packet,
Sister and Brother making a racket.
Cornflakes and toast if we have bread,
snotty noses wiped and off to school we head.

Just missed the solo in the school choir
running home in tears tripping in the mire.
Just missed being Mary in the nativity,
'You can be narrator with your photographic memory.

Rummaging through jumble sales,

washing clothes in the bath.

Dad is acting silly and they are having a laugh.

Burning old shoes during the miners strikes.

No warmth to be had as we huddle round the fire,

the stink of burning rubber as the flames leap higher.

Running to the shop to buy candles for the night.

Rivers mountains and streams played by candlelight.

A serial joiner, of every church and group in town,

I remember telling Mum, and how she used to frown.

I would head off to Sunday school, Mum and Dad still in bed.

I just could not wait for those Bible stories to be read.

Christmas time, draft sherry and port,

Dad's few bottles of beer bought.

Toffees on the tree, the snow globe on the hearth.

Nylon nighties changed into before lunch,

a bagful of nuts on which to munch.

Mum and Dad happy for that one day in the year,

children hoping the atmosphere would never disappear.

Children are now grown up and gone.

We never had much of any real value,

except our memories which remain clear and true.

© 2018 Taylor Crowshaw

Your Beauty

Your smile immortalised upon the paper.
Grey quickly sketched lines,
features pure and fine.

Your lips part in expectation,
of the kiss... for which you are waiting.

Unaware of the effect your beauty holds,
those lines so quickly drawn unfold.
A love born of passion,
almost going out of fashion.

From hand to pencil to paper,
loves intensity laboured.

Admiring your image after so many years,
emotion now moving me to tears.
A miracle that this drawing still exists.
The question...
Was that kiss ever placed upon your lips?

© 2018 Taylor Crowshaw

Lies

The dying embers of the fire
gave their faces a luminescence.
Their need visible, one to the other.

Lies bubbled forth spewing out,
unable to be contained as if their very corruption caused a reflexive
response.
The speaker of the lies throwing each one as far away as possible from
the responsibility of having told that lie,
as if the lie and the teller can be separated by distance.

The receiver of the lie eating them up with a hunger born of desperation,
needing the reassurance of those falsehoods.
Needing to go on, each lie greedily devoured.
Filling their empty belly, contenting it as it is slowly digested bringing a
stuporous rest.
Easing the pangs which had beset them from... that day.

The lie is heavy now in the room,

both a wanted and unwanted guest, who can never be uninvited.

Forever spoken,

it sits between them,

and they know.

© 2018 Taylor Crowshaw

Crooked Wing

She has a broken wing
but still she can sing.
Hiding in the dark
she held her broken wing.

She had a broken heart
it was torn apart,
by the singing of the Lark...
She nursed her broken heart.

She had a broken life
a mother and a wife.
Such sorrow and strife
she mourned her broken life.

It is time to move on
all hoping is now done,
the past a barren land
taken from her hand.

Her broken wing now healed,

its crookedness revealed.

The memories will fade,

as the future is now played.

© 2018 Taylor Crowshaw

The Tall Pines

Puffs of powdered snow fall from the tall pine tree,
a crow's nest atop it sits precariously.
Breath exhaled evaporating into steam,
the beauty of it almost a dream.

The hedgehog now long asleep beneath the twigs and leaves.
Acorns stored and ready to be exhumed,
a squirrel's hearty meal soon will be consumed.
The squirrels huddle in their den,
popping out to eat every now and then.

A red deer grunts nostril flaring wide,
velvety antlers still unshed crowning his glory as he strides.
Slowly he disappears among the pines,
a majestic ghostly figure in his prime.

Birds flitter here and there waxy berries bright and alluring.
Feasting heartily on their meal,
with an enthusiasm they cannot conceal.

The smell of pine needles underneath my feet,
fresh as the dawn of each day that we greet.

Beauty surrounds me in the tall pines, a clear blue ceiling
above a white carpeted floor.
Where a world of wonder lies beyond the forest floor.

The soft hooting of the owl as it watches taking in all,
a hawk's screaming echoing call.

With the eyes of a child you can look in awe,
a world not seen by the ordinary eye.
With the innocence of a child, and their uncluttered mind,
they can see wonders of every kind.

The feather which flutters... to them is not a feather,
it's another item for their box of treasure.
A shell so out of place on a forest floor,
must have been brought here from some distant shore.
Ahh... the pine cone that beckons them,
to be coloured by their pen,
hung up on their Christmas tree,
a beautiful present from them to me.

Wandering home hand in hand,
passing through this magical land.

The children shout their departing cry...

"Goodbye pines standing tall and proud,

we will be back again, as soon as we're allowed."

© 2018 Taylor Crowshaw

Dad

Twenty-one national service done.
Boxing and skiing near Trieste,
an Italian uniform on parade,
you can be sure he was not afraid.

Appendix out at thirty-five.
A hospital visit,
dad stood on his head,
while doing yoga on his bed.

Electric shocks at thirty-seven,
he thought he had died, but it was not heaven.
Two years depressed and mostly in bed.
with us small children stroking his head.

Back to work at thirty-nine,
doing well and feeling fine.

Retired at fifty-five,
happy to be done and still alive.
A dog called Blaze to be his friend
to walk to the beach his mind to mend.

A massive stroke at sixty-five.
Staring at his reflection in the wardrobe mirrors,
watching himself disappear little by little.
His body frail and brittle.

Bedridden to the end,
his family surround him
to his needs they tend.

In his coffin at sixty-nine,
leaving all of us behind.
Memories good and bad.

Upon reflection both happy and sad.

© 2018 Taylor Crowshaw

Rick you were amazing...

Tracks

This was a journey on which I was taken,
where my bones and body were shaken.
On that long and bumpy track,
shattering my tired and worn out back.

Unkempt hedges line the way,
hills and troughs on those lanes.
Rows of fields stacked with hay.

The dappled shade from the summer sun.
Children's laughter having fun,
roars and cheers from some game they've won.

Now we navigate the bog,
stopping to move a broken log.
Bullfinches fly from rush to rush,
I stifle a gasp at this colourful sight,
causing the birds to all take flight.

We pass the lake sun beating down.
Still and polished like a mirror.

Finally, we arrive,

to this place we have been many times before.

Looking at each other we briefly touch hands,

before we knock upon that door.

© 2018 Taylor Crowshaw

This Hill I Sit Atop

A mountain I have climbed
change forever out of reach,
no first night opening speech.
A one-time lullaby,
the sound of a child's cry.
Fading into the night
hope has taken flight,
no darkness into light.
No strength to stay and fight.
A well of unshed tears,
consciousness choked with fear.
Hiding in my room,
a comfortable tomb.

© 2018 Taylor Crowshaw

The Emptiness

This wonderful thing called birth,

this beauteous child you have delivered onto this earth.

Bitter sweet sorrow filling your heart a tremendous gap of which they were

a part.

This life to which your life is dedicated,

this life which you have both created.

No longer a part of you but still a part of your heart,

torn cruelly from your body before you were ready to be apart.

Why can they not understand this emptiness you feel?

Even though you see her lying in her cradle,

you are not ready to let go yet… she is still you it is still we.

This is a time of readjustment they say,

looking at you and then quickly away.

Not knowing the sorrow you feel, the emptiness inside,

the tears you cannot hide.

She smiles at others not only you.

You feel a twinge of jealousy.

The days roll on and that feeling has evaporated,

but still a sorrow lingers an emptiness.

Until you see her smile, you hold her, and you are grateful.

© 2018 Taylor Crowshaw

The Girl

I always thought of myself as a roses kind of girl,

but you brought me daffodils.

I always thought of myself as a diamond kind of girl,

but you brought me Chanel perfume.

I always thought of myself as silk negligee kind of girl,

but you brought me pretty underwear.

I always thought of myself as a box of chocolates type of girl,

but you brought me a Christmas tree.

You have always known me... better than I know me.

© 2018 Taylor Crowshaw

A Fresh Start is the Best Start

Not easy with so many anchors.
Grandchildren like tendrils from the root,
directly for our hearts they shroot.

Telling me they have a plan,
to sabotage our own plans.
A messy house for prospective buyers.
Or upon our departure letting down our tyres.

I watched your parents as they grew,
now each day I watch you too.
It's time to leave now,
time for us to take a bow.

We need to steal some time for ourselves,
to sit and take a breath,
before we both welcome death.

Our home is yours wherever we are,
you can reach it easily... it won't be too far.
Better to have us well... somewhere else.
Than be ashes in a jar sat on your shelf.

© 2018 Taylor Crowshaw

Midnight

I would often sit and ponder,

what would it be like to have a mind that didn't wander.

To be at peace with myself,

not the internal wars that sit ready on the shelf.

Waiting to raise their ugly heads,

just as I settle into my bed.

Shadows crouch in the gloom,

waiting to pounce creating a sense of doom.

I shuffle and turn this way and that.

Perhaps that shadow is my hat.

Cursed with an imagination that runs wild,

my unfortunate gift even as a child.

The dark shadows... the mist that swirls,

those tendrils that make my mind unfurl.

The shadows retreat as daylight dawns,

fears set back down, hope reborn.

My mind still racing far ahead,

fearing the inevitable return to my bed.

© 2018 Taylor Crowshaw

A Sense of Identity

There you are identity for years you have hidden from me,
I had my life neatly in a box
until that day when you were lost.

A father difficult but much loved.
A mother true identity unknown.
A mask really only ever shown.

Out of the blue the rug was pulled from under me,
why could she not have let things be?
Lost my heritage, my past a lie.
She was itching to tell us I didn't know why.

Ahh!!!, but her lover had returned,
and his love for us had to be earned.
Anger, rage, beat this mind and body of mine.
Love to be earned? I had no time.

The anchor of parents is our stability.
When the anchor is pulled up we are cast adrift.
Left lost and alone in a sea of confusion and doubt,
difficult to let our feelings out.

Looking into a mirror seeing someone who you do not know,

'She looks just like her dad.'

people would say.

What were they thinking they must all be mad.

Eventually we had to let it go,

just too much baggage to tow.

Forgive and move on.

One day, who knows. We may have been friends.

© 2018 Taylor Crowshaw

I Want

Do you remember playing by the gate?

Those precious moments that would not wait,

the plays that we would put on.

Sad to say those days have gone.

Do you remember playing in our den?

I want to be that child again.

Do you remember our first kiss?

Those moments that we missed,

how bright our futures were back then.

I want to have my youth again.

Do you remember our first child?

How my music drove you wild.

My dancing to the latest tunes,

you laughed and called me a loon.

Do you remember when you lost your mother?

That day was to you as no other.

Do you remember when you lost your twin?

No more games for you to win.

I don't want you to suffer such loss again.

Do you remember your first daughter's marriage?

You sat holding her hand in the carriage.

You hold her child so like her,

a halo of curly golden hair.

I remember all of the above.

It's locked away in my heart encased in love.

© 2018 Taylor Crowshaw

Love an Island Seldom Visited

Sails on the breeze of a lost lover's seas.

Love's desires burn body and heart.

Minds consumed obsessed,

the fire a matter yet to be addressed.

A distant shore comes into focus only to be pushed away,

mundanity to be dealt with on another day.

Waves crash the shore of our desire,

a clichéd movie score,

passion soaring ever higher.

Sailing away from that ghostly isle,

to rest in each other's arms still a little while.

This island seldom visited may call us again to its distant shores,

just as it beckoned us many years before.

© 2018 Taylor Crowshaw

The Matriarch

Swaying gently in the breeze,
I am one of the tall pine trees.
Needles fall like rain,
upon the forest's counterpane.

Cones like hailstones to the ground.
The forest animals alert to every sound.
Stirrings from the forest floor,
I wait to oversee proceedings,
a performance which I am leading.

You dare to sit on my branches birds.
I shake you off, you flock,
as if you dare to mock.

The shadow which I cast afar,
reaching upwards to the stars.

I am the overseer,
the matriarch.
The immense tower of bark.

My roots an anchor from the wind,

my branches home to those with wings.

I have stood for decades here,

the forest over which I preside,

the creatures who use my trees to hide.

This forest of pine... dozy but never completely asleep.

Throughout the seasons we can see,

the comings and goings amongst the trees.

Stand I will for decades more,

until finally my time will come.

When I will hear the deafening roar,

and the machine will arrive with its mighty saw.

© 2018 Taylor Crowshaw

The 500 Piece Jigsaw that is Me

Pieces fall away deconstructing me one piece at a time.

A death 499 pieces

A divorce 498 pieces

A move 497 pieces

Slowly disappearing into oblivion one piece at a time.

© 2018 Taylor Crowshaw

Sunset

Sat, legs dangling over the rock she watches.

The sunset casts its reflection on a calm sea,

aflame with red and orange hues,

she stretches then bends to retrieve her shoes.

The sound of the waves gently washing the shore,

as she lays down to stay just a few minutes more.

A velvety warmth... remnants of a scorching hot day,

envelops her body as on the rock she lay.

Alone with her thoughts she is drifting to sleep,

the tears held at bay as she tries not to weep.

Rising she stares far out to sea,

so many questions, so much to see.

The time has come for her to go,

as she puts on her shoes nice and slow.

Leaving this place which had once been her home.

Days which had once been so easy and slow,

into a future which she does not know.

Turning once more she falls to her knees.

Picking up the sand which runs through her fingers with ease.

Images play like an old movie in her mind's eye,

small children build sandcastles with a moat,

while her brother is in the sea trying to float.

Her children and grandchildren had played there too.

She watched from the shore as they swam in the sea.

Now as she watches from her special rock,

they disappear from sight in the blink of an eye,

an old movie reel spinning, she can't understand why.

Time seems tangled confused and unclear,

but she still hears the sound of the sea rushing… in her ears.

© 2018 Taylor Crowshaw

A Moment in my Mind

A million moments captured,

precious dewdrops of time.

Our child's first breath our parents last.

A first kiss

a smile.

Preserved In our minds eye until that moment when we die,

but we were captured in another's eye and so we continue until they die.

® 2018 Taylor Crowshaw

Moon Shadows

I saw through eyes shining with unshed tears,

a shadowy figure, still waiting.

My heart heavy with sorrow for what could have been.

Dreams of yesterday held within a mind of today.

Lost in a maze of confusion and doubts, silently screaming.

I am a land vast, empty, void, a barren wasteland.

Shadows lurk waiting for the weak to fall.

I cannot fall, for if I fall it is the end… the emptiness will always remain.

The shadow will pass over me consuming me as it drifts across our lives.

Questions cannot be answered if there is no one to ask,

it is a question of identity.

I remain identity unknown.

© 2018 Taylor Crowshaw

Come and See Me Before I Die

I have never asked you much for if I do you always sigh,
but I would ask this of you, come and see me before I die.

You all ask me why it is I cry,
I would just say come and see me before I die.

When you leave after a visit, I have tears in my eyes.
You ask what's wrong, I reply. "Come and see me before I die."

You may think I'm selfish and ask yourself why,
I am always asking you to see me before I die.

You will one day realise that that was never true,
and that the reason I asked… was not for me but for you.

© 2018 Taylor Crowshaw

A Kindness

So easily delivered the soft touch of a hand a smile,
a smile so much less effort than a frown.
Soft words,
not the harsh barrage of criticism
delivered because you can.

Thinking your sharp wit amusing,
a knife which cuts deeper with each thrust.
What do we do other than acquiesce.
Ahh but one should never be kind or gentle.
This world is not for the gentle or kind, it is for others.

We remain.
Radios to be tuned in,
to be switched off at the slightest suggestion of resistance,
waiting… a life spent waiting for a kindness to be performed,
a worm which turned no longer is required.
If we ask… why… you would just say… "What about you?"

How many doors were open to us, forks in the road to choose.
Those forks not our forks, those roads not our roads.
We are passengers on somebody else's journey.
I am but one of many who travel these same paths.

Held fast by a sorrow not for ourselves but for you.

The cord by which we are attached,

the umbilicus from which you feed.

My passion never faltered it played its rhythmic tune,

but yours my love a flame extinguished far too soon.

You are blind you do not see.

These words bleed... from the open wound that is me.

© 2018 Taylor Crowshaw

The Old Vanity Case

She stood and watched the tram disappear,
a young child whose body was now rigid with fear.

Every week she went off to ballet on the tram,
with a half a crown, which she got from her mam.

They had practiced today for their latest show.
What she would do now she did not know,
as she watched the tram departing easy and slow.

For on a seat alone on that tram,
her vanity case sits forlorn and forgotten.
Leaving that poor child feeling frightened and rotten.

Slowly she trudges her way back home.
The old cobbled street feels hard on her tired feet,
but that day she did not notice, when her mother she did meet.

The first thing mother notices are her empty hands,
"Where is your vanity case?" her mother demands.
She points into the distance and sees the tram disappear,
before she suddenly receives a hard slap on her rear.

She was never to go to ballet again.

With tear stained cheeks she sits at her bedroom window.

She spends her days watching those trams rumble by,

and wonders who took her place in that show.

© 2018 Taylor Crowshaw

Broken

Far into the woods she sits all alone,
unaware of a stranger who knows she is there,
she shivers and holds her arms which are fragile and bare.

Hair hanging over her eyes as her head is bowed,
her sobbing and weeping hollow and loud.
The cry of a wolf alone in the dark,
a fox's eerily echoing bark.

Skirt brushing the dry leaves as she walks,
the sound of her words to herself as she talks.
Her step is unsure faltering every now and then,
but she picks herself up and starts walking again.

Throbbing and full she feels her head will explode
or failing that, her whole being will implode.

The door no longer ajar as she watches from afar,
closed to her now nothing left to receive.
The loss of a life for which she does not grieve.

A life sacrificed for others with nothing but pain,
no longer needed by them who have no more to gain.
The stranger still watches through his veil of tears.
As he sees the old woman broken alone,
his love by whom he was rejected for years.

He remembers days past her light touch on his arm,
how her smile his resolve would always disarm.
She was swept away by another's passion,
his love to her then had seemed old and unfashioned.

Both had looked longingly back on those days,
they were innocents then in so many ways.
Regrets were a mountain that they could not climb,
a mountain, which had grown over time.

Her love for the stranger had always stayed strong,
although in her heart she knew this was wrong.
She had sent him away time after time,
whilst wishing into his arms she could climb.

He ran through the woods like the young man he once was,
to help his love who was lost and alone.
She turned and looked behind as she heard the branch break,
shaking her head to make sure she was awake.

As they stood looking at each other from across the way.

The passage of time and the years fell away.

They were found together on a soft bed of leaves.

Smiles on their lifeless faces,

where the trails of their tears had left their traces.

They never discovered where the young lovers came from that day,

or why their beloved mother had run far away.

© 2018 Taylor Crowshaw

Time To Let Go

The time has gone for being smart,
having no heart
for taking part.

The time has gone for chasing gain,
avoiding rain
being ashamed.

The time has gone for building debts,
having regrets
placing bets.

The time has gone for raising kids,
being on the skids
time to be rid.

The time has come for you and me,
time to be free
by the sea.

© 2018 Taylor Crowshaw

Following

I follow the path that leads me to you,
hesitation pulling me from a love bright and new.
A lifetime of regrets weighs heavy inside,
a past from which I can no longer hide.

Drawn together from either side of the lake,
to deny our love would be a mistake.
You glance over at me
and me back to you.

Flushed and flustered I do not respond,
but you know in your heart
to you I belong.

When finally, we meet,
our love which we greet.
All hesitation now forgotten and gone,
together our hearts beat as one.

You came to me with an open heart,

offering your love and a new start.

I am still that young woman.

You are still that young man.

Our love for each other a lifetime will span.

© 2018 Taylor Crowshaw

My Life

Tied to others having huge responsibilities.
Work which was never shirked.
Children loved and raised,
a trail through life was blazed.

Slowly letting each one of them go,
not easy but better when done nice and slow.

Now it's our time my time I am your wife,
but remember....
I don't want to live your version of my life.

© 2018 Taylor Crowshaw

The following two poems were written when I discovered that the man who had raised me was not my biological father.

My mother had been in love as a young woman, but that young man was driven away by her parents. He went off to join the military police in Hong Kong where he served for over 6 years.

During this time my mother married my father and had a baby boy.

Upon the young man's return they resumed their relationship, which continued all throughout her marriage producing two children, myself and my sister.

My father was a beautiful loving and caring man who I deeply adored.

However, he was a gambler and from the age of 36 suffered from a depressive form of schizophrenia.

My mother worked hard paid the mortgage, raised a family and gave my father a normal
life. Nursing him for four long years, after a massive stroke left him bedridden for the majority of time.

On his deathbed he acknowledged her sacrifice. She had been closed indoors with my father who smoked heavily for four long years. He was just 69 when he died.

My mother met up with my biological father after my dad had died and they decided to tell us the truth and try to make up for their years apart.

Unfortunately, after two years my mother was diagnosed with lung cancer and after a four year struggle she died aged 69. My biological father lost the will to go on and died just over 18 months later.

I have no regrets about my young life with my father even though it was very difficult at times. My father and I were very close.

The only thing I would say is that my mother and my biological father should not have told us that we were not dads' children. I believe she thought it would cement their relationship, and we would be the happy family she had always dreamed of. However, this man already had 6 other children. We were in our forties at that stage and all he really wanted was his lover not to bond with children he did not know. All it achieved was to rob us of our identity leading to many years of confusion. We have come to terms with it and it never affected our love for our father, or our relationship with our mother and biological father who were both wonderful people.

The first poem was written over 19 years ago when I first found out in 1999. The second poem was written this year 2018.

If you wish to know more... there us so much more to know.
My autobiographical book of poetry is available on Amazon.
Shhhh!!!! We Don't Talk About That by Taylor Crowshaw.

Enjoy the poems. Thank you for reading. Taylor

Your Story

Guilty secrets precious moments,
locked away in the deep recesses of hearts and minds.
Unlocked during brief moments,
to be touched by tendrils afraid to feel,
pushed deeper inside.

Hidden from sight,
brick upon brick a wall to shield.
Stoney heart, a mask unnatural unwanted, necessary.

Two precious buds unaware of their beginnings,
growing striving.
Eyes watching yearning reaching.
Hope buried deep, fear a constant companion.
Emotions running on parallel lines crisscrossing
through the years.

Roots anchored in a sandy bed, unsteady, shallow.
Cruelly torn out, searching, clinging.
Gingerly tender shoots move blindly toward more solid ground.
Hope blossoms unfolding its petals, innocently
exposing itself.

Flinching under a searing sun,
salty tears scorch and burn.

Steadying arms enfold, lovingly tender.
A heart begins to beat again softening,
daring in the autumn of their lives... to seek and find a place to dwell.

© 1999 Taylor Crowshaw

Their Love was a Beacon

To her their love was all...

A lighthouse a shining beacon upon the tumultuous sea which was her life.

It kept her steering a steady ship through the cruel years.

Keeping her afloat and saving her from drowning, crashing upon the rocks.

I did not condemn or condone... I understood.

© 2018 Taylor Crowshaw

Part Two - A Humorous Break

Never Stop

I will never stop loving you
never stop being true,
never stop having a laugh
or having a bath.

I will never stop playing the fool,
never stop thinking myself cool
sticking to the rules
using your tools.

I will never stop loving life
stop being your wife
giving you strife,
all of my life.

© 2018 Taylor Crowshaw

A Dip

We went on a trip
to the shore to take a dip.

We saw a small dog chasing a stick.
His owner thought it quite a joke
to replace it with a brick.

The little dog stood staring
at the little brick,
he wondered how it had managed to
change from a stick.

It gave him quite a shock...
So, before his owner found him
he changed it to a rock.

© 2018 Taylor Crowshaw

The Hat

When I was a child

my imagination would run wild.

It was hard to control,

I dreamt my sister was a mole.

I thought I had it beat,

and would buy myself a treat.

At the shop counter I saw a lady in a hat.

I was sure she was concealing a small cricket bat.

When she removed it, what I saw instead,

was that this poor old lady had a rather large head.

I had to control myself...

put my imagination back on the shelf.

Oh no... oh dear... what am I to do?

I think that man over there... has a shovel in his shoe.

© 2018 Taylor Crowshaw

Hell

My friend went on holiday.
She rang me from Poland today.

I asked her was she enjoying her stay.
She told me there was a place called Hell,
and that she knew it very well.

She told me the only reason she had gone away,
to visit Poland and there to stay,
was so that she would be able to say.
I have been to Hell and back today.

© 2018 Taylor Crowshaw

The Boy Who Was a Funiosity

The boy they called a funiosity
whose downfall was his curiosity.
He jumped into a box full of shoes
and got shipped off to Peru.

When they found him, they said he could have been cleaner,
before they sent him down to Lima.
He thought it was all terrific,
and hopped on a ship to cross the Pacific.

He was quite peculiar, in his own amusing style,
wearing a panama hat and a great big smile.
In his mind was an idea to see the glacial melt
where the Atlantic meets the Pacific would be exciting so he felt.

He sailed away on that ship,
where the Captain beat his crew with a whip.
He would hide away in the hold,
he was no coward, but he was not bold.

When they arrived at their destination

where the glacial melt underwent creation.

He ended up in the drink,

and that was the end of him... I think.

© 2018 Taylor Crowshaw

Nan's Lippy

Nanna she was young at heart.

It's hard to know where to start.

She always was a lively girl,

loved to dance and to whirl.

When she started having trouble with her sight.

She just could not get her lipstick right,

it was everywhere else on her face.

Other than her lips where there was no trace.

Eventually one of her eyes they had to remove,

but even that did not stop her groove.

She never grew old in my eyes,

but where she wore her lippy was always a surprise.

© 2018 Taylor Crowshaw

Noodles

When we got little Noodles home we were quite delighted,
even when from the kitchen table she alighted.
The next day when I turned around,
I thought I would see her on the ground.
There she was on the garden wall,
we were afraid she would have a fall.

The breeder said she had a good pedigree,
and that we could buy her for a fee.
We were told she was a spaniel,
and very easy to handle.

I was quite shocked when she went into a tray to do a poo,
I had always thought dogs went into the garden to the loo.

She always jumps from the window sill onto the table.
We used to be afraid but now we know she is quite able.

When I called her earlier she was chasing a mouse around the stable.

Instead of going to the park to play with friends and have a chat,
she would rather sunbathe with the next door neighbours cat.
We love her very much so please do not be fooled,
even though on my best bedding she does often drool.

As I stand here and watch her sitting on the matt,
I think we must have accidentally bought an ugly cat.

© 2018 Taylor Crowshaw

Too Short for Shorts

Knee length, calf length, short shorts.
The question is how to deport,
in your pair of shorts.

Blue, green, yellow, every colour under the sun.
I wonder how they will fit my bum.

Twigs for legs sticking out, I'm hardly likely to
get a whistle or shout.
A chicken has better knees than me.
I think I need a cup of tea.

Gazing into the full-length mirror.
I think I need Botox and a bit of filler.
I turn around to admire my behind,
there is quite a lot to admire I find.

I ask, "Are these shorts a good idea?"
You point out my height and then disappear.
Perhaps, If I wear a pair of heels or courts...
but at five foot two I fear I'm too short for shorts.

© 2018 Taylor Crowshaw

The Rather Large Whale

In the deep blue sea, there lives a large whale,

and of him and his friend this is a small tale.

He was a creature of devotion,

who roamed around the ocean.

His friend, the tiny squid

was always good for a quid.

They were the best of friends even tho the whale was big

but he never did like… the squid's big purple wig.

© 2018 Taylor Crowshaw

Drama

Sitting cosy in the evening in my armchair,

I can never help it, but at the TV I do stare.

I feel I am addicted to my favourite soap,

that if I do not get my fix how will I ever cope.

My favourite character has just been killed off,

I think he's buried in the garden underneath a trough.

Cheryl's just gone missing with Suzie's husband John.

The private detective is trying to find out where they have gone.

The adverts signal much manic activity,

quick let's get some biccies and a cup of tea.

Shhhh its back on...arms waving fingers to lips,

husband throwing out sarcastic quips.

Trudi's had her baby they have named him Paul.

They do say his dad's not Jack they think that it's Saul.

The scene cuts to a courtroom,

atmosphere oppressive all doom.

Camera zooms into the foreman of the jury,

swinging back to the defendant eyes wide and wild.

How will he manage if he loses his child?

Credits start to roll before the verdict is delivered.

I cannot help reflecting how much is in the plot,

and wonder how they manage, to fit it all into a thirty-minute slot.

© 2018 Taylor Crowshaw

Part Three - Various Creatures

Beyond the Trees

Beyond the trees in a deep dark hole,
lives a fox and his friend the mole.
The mole did not know that his friend ate mole meat,
for he could see no further than his feet.

The mole brought the fox a gift of worms,
which managed to keep them on good terms.
Although the fox's glance would have told a different tale,
had Mr. Mole been able to surveil.

A winter chill swept through their den,
the fox began to feel hungry again.
Now the mole certainly was no fool,
and realised he needed to keep his cool.

If he could find no more worms,
how would he keep them on good terms?
When he pushed his nose up through the ground,
this is what the little mole found.

He heard a noise right under a log,

and there he found a juicy frog.

Off he went with his gift,

he knew it would give his friend a lift.

The fox enjoyed his juicy frog,

which mole had found under a log.

He was so happy that in return,

he gave his friend the mole a juicy worm.

This tale is fraught with danger for the mole,

the situation is beyond his control.

There sits in the den an uneasy truce,

unless the fox's natural instincts are let loose.

So, the mole never rests for more than ten,

while the fox lies slumbering in the den.

© 2018 Taylor Crowshaw

The Fledgling

I hear your persistent call,
as you sit upon that crumbling wall.
Softly feathered tiny bird,
it's time to go have you not heard.

The nest is but a memory,
as you follow your parents from tree to tree.
"Hey mum hey dad come on feed me,
I'm hungry now I need my tea."

A juicy bug crawls on the ground,
you approach it carefully without a sound.
Gobbling him up is no bother,
as overhead your parents hover.

Your confidence begins to grow.
You no longer need mum and dad in tow.
Off into the world you fly,
disappearing into the bright blue sky.

© 2018 Taylor Crowshaw

Mrs Prickles

When I went into the stable what did I find?
A hedgehog rolled into a ball on the ground.
Barney the dog was curled up in his bed.
How had that intruder got into the shed?

Cautiously I picked her up she was quite a big girl,
she was not willing her body to unfurl.
Barney sniffed but backed off pretty quick.,
tthose pesky prickles gave his nose a nasty prick...

Lifting her gently I put her in a box,
I left her some dog food and water for her tea,
Barney watched on as he sat by my knee.

We left her for a while those delicious smells wafting around.
Peeping into the box trying not to make a sound.
Little shiny eyes looked straight up at me,
I almost imagined she was thanking me for her tea.

Fed and watered it was time for her to go,

I tipped up the box nice and slow.

She hesitated briefly before moving away,

we have never seen her since right up to this day.

© 2018 Taylor Crowshaw

The Fox Visited Me Last Night

Soft brown eyes tonight, colour the night
a flash of white tail, as you take flight.

Stealthily you come to me.

Nose in the air as unfamiliar scents waft by,
a full moon guiding you from on high.
Ears alert to every sound.
Soft paws pad through the undergrowth,
making heir way to more solid ground.

Always ready to retreat and disappear into the night.

Your life a battle to survive,
a constant will to stay alive.

Your bark so shrill, gives me a chill.
I wonder where you are,
are you here with me still?

© 2018 Taylor Crowshaw

Montague

Purring cat with ginger fur,
just how long have you been there?

Silently watching my every move.
Is it time to leave you food?
All these years you have watched the world pass by,
with your head heavy you give a sigh.

Birds no longer scatter when you are around.
They just continue picking things up from the ground.
I don't find carcasses or presents at the door,
you have no need to prove your worth any more.

Your friends have all gone there is only you,
before long, it will be your time too.

Don't let that stop you dreaming of the chase.
I can still appreciate the beauty of your face.
Rest my little one, stretch out in the sun,
there is still life there is still fun.

© 2018 Taylor Crowshaw

The Den

Little wren,
do you have a den?

As the twilight begins to fall,
I can hear your signalling call.
You all start to appear.
It's time to settle down this is clear.

A tiny crack beside the window is your den,
you all pile in I counted nine or ten.
Jostling for position space is tight,
snug and warm for the night.

Roosting together until daylight,
when you all depart taking flight.
Going on your separate ways.
Until you all meet up again, at the end of the day.

© 2018 Taylor Crowshaw

Under the Stairs

See through spider are you there
hiding underneath the stairs?
Your offspring tiny but just like you.
Hundreds of them all see through.

When my children see you they start to shiver,
as your web begins to quiver.
Legs like silk fine and long.
Under the stairs is where you belong.

Your hiding place will be quite safe.
Do not be foolish and venture out,
lest my children begin to shout.

The hoover looms large in the room,
please stay hidden in the gloom.
You are doing no harm there...
Hidden underneath the stairs.

© 2018 Taylor Crowshaw

Funny Little Dog

You my little Chinese Dragon.

You of the boggley eyes.

You who were my **S**urprise.

Tiny dog with a curly tail.

Tiny dog whose charm never fails.

Tiny dog with the **H**eart of a lion.

Shitzu crossed with Bichon Frieze.

Shitzu who loves the trees.

Shitzu who never begs ple**A**se.

Big dog but a little girl.

Big dog who likes to ru**N** and twirl.

Big dog in a tiny body.

You rule the roost in our home.

You rule the yar**D** and never moan.

You rule the mobile telephone.

A rather large character.

A rather large taker of m**Y** chair.

A rather large head of hair.

© 2018 Taylor Crowshaw

The Dawn

I stood in the garden at the breaking of dawn,
stretching my arms wide and releasing a yawn.
A small flittering creature swooped and flew around the shed,
I ducked very quickly protecting my head.

I searched above in the pale daylight,
every now and then catching a glimpse from the corner of my eye,
as the small creature swooped and then continued to fly.

He sensed but did not see my presence.
His radar finely tuned to detect any object that stood in his way,
I was a mountain to his tiny form, as I stood in the garden that day.

For he was ready to sleep all during the day,
the only problem being, that I stood in his way.

I retreated from the garden, no longer static,
so that the tiny young bat could sleep in the attic.

© 2018 Taylor Crowshaw

You Wore a Path

Over the years through the seasons, you trod your path,
in single file across the field you wore your way,
back into the stable yard every single day.

Long ears soft coat and gentle faces,
my friends of heart and home.
The comfort you gave in times of stress,
although you could make quite a mess.

Calm stubborn intelligent creatures,
handsome and fine with wonderful features.
You chase each other around the field,
but little donkeys you will not yield.

Escaping is your speciality,
I chase you all around the trees,
huffing and puffing while you run with ease.

What can I give you for all you've given me?
except a thank you and a home where you can be… happy.
You wore a path in the field, but that is only a part,
you all wore a deeper path right across my heart.

© 2018 Taylor Crowshaw

The King of Inishturk

I heard tell of a donkey,
The King of Inishturk.
At 27 years old he no longer works.
He roams the island, wild and proud and free,
this good old boy is as happy as he could ever be.

The last remaining donkey on the Isle of Inishturk.

Adopted by those all around,
the King's forever home is bound.
Clifftop he surveys the shore.
Mountainside the land.
This is his sanctuary,
The Isle of Inishturk.

He wanders through his kingdom
through sun, and snow and rain.
Throughout each season his dignity he maintains.

The sheep of the moors his company,
the people are his guests,
bow now to the King before he takes his rest.

Watch for this solitary figure wandering the shore.

For such an honour it will be,

if you are fortunate enough to see.

The last remaining donkey on the Isle of Inishturk.

© 2018 Taylor Crowshaw

He is the last remaining donkey on this beautiful island off the coast of

Mayo in Ireland.

My name is Taylor Crowshaw

I was born in 1959 in Fleetwood a small fishing town in the Northwest of England.
I relocated to Ireland in 1994 with my children, husband Peter and our two dogs at the time, Sally and Sophie. I am mother to ten wonderful children, grandmother to twenty grandchildren and great grandmother to one.

I live on a smallholding surrounded by a beautiful pine forest. Together with my husband Peter, my youngest daughter Fleur. 5 donkeys, 4 dogs, 1 cat and numerous chickens.

Thank you for reading The Slumbering Pines.

Taylor

Other publications available on Amazon by Taylor Crowshaw:

- *Shhhh!!!! We Don't Talk About That*
- *The Tracings Of My Shadow*

10722784R00058

Printed in Great Britain
by Amazon